D1528893

THE GREAT AMERICAN
BUNION DERBY

Molly Levite Griffis
Researched by Jim Ross

EAKIN PRESS ✦ Austin, Texas

FIRST EDITION
Copyright © 2003
By Molly Levite Griffis
Published in the United States of America
By Eakin Press
A Division of Sunbelt Media, Inc.
P.O. Drawer 90159 Austin, Texas 78709-0159
email: sales@eakinpress.com
 website: www.eakinpress.com
ALL RIGHTS RESERVED.
1   2   3   4   5   6   7   8   9
1-57168-801-3 HB
1-57168-810-2 PB

Library of Congress Cataloging-in-Publication Data

Griffis, Molly Levite.
    The Great American bunion derby / Molly Levite Griffis.– 1st ed.
        p.   cm.
    Summary: A biography of Andrew Hartley Payne which focuses on his partici-
pation in the 1928 International Trans-Continental Foot Race, in which he won
the title of "The Best Long Distance Runner in the World."
    ISBN 1-57168-801-3 (alk. paper)
    1. Payne, Andrew Hartley, 1907-1977–Juvenile literature. 2 Runners (Sports)
–United States–Biography–Juvenile literature. 3. Cherokee Indians–Biography–
Juvenile literature. 4. Indians of North America–Biography–Juvenile literature.
[1. Payne, Andrew Hartley, 1907-1977. 2. Runners (Sports) 3. Marathon running. 4. Running races. 5. Cherokee Indians–Biography. 6. Indians of North
America–Biography.] I. Title
GV1061.15.P39G75 2003
796.42'092–dc21   2003008817

In *Through the Looking Glass* by
Lewis Carroll, the queen observed:
"Now, here, you see, it takes all the running
you can do, to keep in the same place.
If you want to get somewhere else, you
must run at least twice as fast as that!"

In the spring of 1928,
Andy Payne, part Cherokee Indian
from Foyil, Oklahoma,
who wanted very badly to
"get somewhere else,"
said the same thing.
Only Andy said it with his feet.

For
John Jacobs
University of Oklahoma Track Coach
1922–1965

Harold Keith
University of Oklahoma Sports Information Director
1930–1969

and

Bill Connors
Tulsa World Sports Writer
1952–2000

"Twice as fast runners" all.

Contents

Acknowledgments   vii

1-Foot Power   1

2-The Longest Footrace Ever   5

3-Andy's Spiel   11

4-Wings on His Feet   15

5-Nature's Soft Nurse   22

6-The Twice-as-Fast Runner   26

7-Sob-Story Pictures   29

8-Don't Tell 'Em   37

9-Unexpected Pleasures   42

10-Favorite Son   46

11-Cherokee Kid   51

12-The Iron Man   61

13-Good as Gold   70

14-Runner's Heart   74

Afterword   80

Andy Ever After   83

Author's Note   85

About the Author   87

Acknowledgments

This book could have never come to life without the generous help and cooperation of Andy Payne's family. His wife, Vivian, and his daughter, Norma Roupe, both of Oklahoma City, opened their hearts and homes to us, and for that we are very grateful. The trust they put in us by loaning their family treasures both amazed and delighted us. The Paynes' longtime family friend Carolyn Kennedy was also of invaluable help in organizing and arranging the volumes of Payne materials.

While time, distance, and death prevented us from interviewing any of the actual runners involved in the First Annual International Trans-Continental Foot Race (otherwise known as "The Bunion Derby"), we were fortunate enough to find runners who were willing to share their knowledge and experience. Bill Jacobs of Seattle, the son of legendary University of Oklahoma track coach John Jacobs, helped research the life and times of Ed "The Shiek" Gardner, the state of Washington's own favorite son. Dick Smethers' warm and wonderful stories of his days as a harrier at the University of Oklahoma inspired us, and the intriguing trophy case filled with his track medals inspired more than one descriptive passage.

Fred Olds, an Oklahoma treasure if there ever was one, not only gave us permission to use the photograph of his Andy Payne statue (thanks to Dr. Mark Lipe for providing the slide!), but also told us enough stories about poor old Elmer McCurdy to fill another book! Sherry McCray and Debby Ware, my computer gurus, kindly and patiently kept me from killing my computer, while the rest of the Park on Main gang cheered me on.

And last, but certainly not least, thanks go to the many runners who participate in the Bunion Derby races run in memory of Andrew Hartley Payne and the other men who showed the world the meaning of the term "runner's heart."

Chapter 1

Foot Power

Andy Payne was a runner. A swift-footed, lickety-split, house-on-fire runner. Why, that boy could run the five miles to school and the five miles back to his daddy's farm and not even have to stop to suck the stitches out of his side. Wasn't any other kid in Limestone School who could run like that. Not in Oowala, Sequoyah, or Foyil, either. Andy got schooled in all those places, too, and he was never tardy once!

In fact, the only time in his life Andy Payne was late was on the day he was born, November 17, 1907. Andy missed being an Oklahoma Statehood Day Baby by a few hours, but since he couldn't even walk yet, much less run, surely that can't be held against him.

When you're one of seven, you *got* to be fast if you don't want to take second table every meal. Second-table kids never get a grab at a drumstick or a pulley bone. Second-table kids get nothing but the north end of a chicken flying south, that's what second-table kids get.

But chickens weren't the reason Andy ran. Horses were. His brothers and sisters rode pokey old glue-footed nags down the road and then clippity-clopped them into the schoolyard, but not Andy. The first time Andy figured out he was faster than every horse his mama Zona and daddy Andrew Payne owned, he started going to school on foot power.

Andy Payne poses for a family snapshot during training for the Bunion Derby in 1928.
—Vivian Payne collection

Andy didn't like anything at all about farm chores, but he liked everything there was about school. Reading and writing. Track meets and running. And after school there was possum hunting and dream-

2

ing. He spent a lot of time dreaming about far-off places, places like California. He heard there were trees in California that sprouted dollar bills instead of leaves. He didn't believe that, of course, but he did believe a state nicknamed "Golden" must have plenty to offer a person who was willing to work hard and dig deep.

Tough times all over the land had put his family in serious money trouble, and they'd had to put a mortgage on their farm. Andy Payne couldn't wait to graduate from high school and earn some money so he could help out. He decided early on that California could make his dreams come true.

Route 66, nicknamed "The Mother of all Roads," ran from Los Angeles, California, to Chicago, Illinois, and snaked right through Andy's hometown of Foyil, Oklahoma, in the process. The summer of 1927, Andy Payne stuck his thumb in the air and rode it all the way to California looking for the "honey pond and the fritter tree" he heard were out there.

As he sat on his suitcase on the side of the road, hoping for a ride, Andy Payne began to dream again. But none of those dreams had anything to do with running. In fact, it never once entered Andy's head that by springtime he'd be running that same highway he was hitchhiking now, running Route 66 from start to finish and then hotfooting it on over to New York City after that. Daydreamer though he was, he never once pictured himself running a three thousand four hundred twenty-three and three-tenth mile footrace. Or, as one math whiz of a sports reporter later figured it, a six million twenty-three thousand two hundred and forty-eight yard dash!

In fact, twenty-year-old Andy Payne, whose Indian heritage had made him a born runner, had to hitchhike all the way from Oklahoma to California to learn he would run that same distance and more before he turned twenty-one.

Chapter 2

The Longest Footrace Ever

California wasn't at all what Andy expected. Oh, it was pretty, all right, pretty and green with lots of trees and flowers he'd only seen in books, but there wasn't any work to speak of, even when a fellow was willing and eager. All he could find were the same kind of odd jobs he ran into back in Oklahoma, not anything that paid much or lasted long. The factories weren't hiring, and he knew for sure that he'd run across the Mojave Desert barefoot before he'd work on a California fruit farm! He spent most of his time reading the newspaper want ads and writing letters to Vivian, the girl he'd left behind.

Finally, on a day when he hardly had two nickels left to rub together or two shoe soles left to pound the pavement, Andy saw an advertisement in the newspaper that popped his eyes as wide as Little Orphan Annie's. It was a full-page announcement for a footrace. Not an ordinary one- or two-mile footrace, but the longest footrace ever to be run. "The First Annual International Trans-Continental Foot Race" it was ballyhooed. Instead of a cinder track, this race would use the roads and highways between Los Angeles, California, and New York City, New York, for its "track" of over three thousand miles!

"How long would it take a body to run three thousand miles?" Andy wondered out loud. "Could anybody do it and live to tell the tale?" It would take a mighty strong pair of legs, a couple of well-tended feet, and more running shoes than he'd ever owned in his entire life to tackle a race like that. The man who won this marathon, the ad proclaimed, would be crowned "The Best Long Distance Runner in the World"!

"Well, I'd hope to shout!" Andy sighed. Then he saw the prizes being offered.

"First prize is *twenty-five thousand dollars*," Andy whispered when his eyes fixed on that amazing five-digit figure. "Twenty-five thousand dollars!" he repeated, yelling loud enough for everybody on the street to hear. Most people he knew were lucky if they made a hundred dollars a month. Andy had graduated from high school with honors, so it didn't take him long to figure out that winning that one race would earn him more money than he could make working for the next ten years! With that kind of cash, he could pay off the mortgage on

The cover of the official program to C. C. Pyle's trans-continental race.
—Vivian Payne collection

his folks' farm, get himself married to Vivian, do anything he darn well pleased for the rest of his life. Or at least until he was an old man of forty or fifty. His feet began to tingle as he read the rules.

The runners would follow the path of the new Route 66, most of which wasn't even paved yet, to its final leg in Chicago. Then they'd switch to other roads and highways and end up in New York City, New York!

Each day of the race, the runners' times would be clocked with a stopwatch. At the end of the day, an official would record the exact hours, minutes, and seconds used up in that day's lap by each individual. Then a record keeper would post the time on a scoreboard. That sounded reasonable enough.

A specific lap length would be run each day—shorter ones for the more difficult-to-run portions of the road, and longer laps for the easier sections. That was good, too. Whoever planned this out had the runners' feet and legs in mind, Andy told himself as he kept on reading.

Anyone caught hitching a ride or taking a shortcut would be disqualified immediately. Had to have that rule, of course. The Paynes were all straight shooters, and Andy would never disgrace his family name by cheating. Not even for twenty-five thousand dollars!

The race was scheduled to begin on Sunday, March 4, 1928, at three-thirty in the afternoon in a place called the Ascot Speedway in Los Angeles. He could find out where that was and rent himself a place to sleep close by. He could pick up enough odd jobs to pay for meals and then spend the rest of his time training, get in lots of hard running before March.

The ad explained there would be a mess tent traveling with the runners to furnish their food, another one to sleep in, and a portable hospital to deal with illnesses or injuries, all "paid for in full by the race management." Free room, board, and medical care the whole time! Those guys had thought of everything.

In the evenings, the runners would be expected to sell programs and visit with the folks in the towns where their tents were pitched for the night. A carnival and sideshow would be traveling with them, so the runners might be asked to give little speeches or entertain up on the stage between acts. Andy wasn't much for public speaking, but he'd muddle through that part somehow. He'd get to meet new people, do new things, and see parts of America he'd never seen before! By the time he finished reading the ad, Andy decided nothing in the world was standing between him and that twenty-five-thousand-dollar first-place finish line!

Then he spotted a hurdle.

A hurdle about as high as Pike's Peak.

An entry fee. An entry fee of twenty-five dollars and a deposit of another one hundred. The deposit would be held in trust as "return-home money" from New York or an earlier spot if the runner dropped out.

Andy sat and stared at those dollar signs for a long time. He'd never seen one hundred twenty-five dollars in one pile in his life, not even on the counter of a teller's cage in a bank.

There was only one place in the world he might be able to come up with that kind of money, and that place was right back where he started from.

Andy Payne packed his suitcase, stuck his thumb in the air again, and headed home to Oklahoma.

Chapter 3

Andy's Spiel

Back home, Andy told the story of the First Annual International Trans-Continental Foot Race so many times he got tired of hearing about it himself. Just having to repeat that title almost wore his tongue out. Even his own father, who was more than certain Andy could win, sidled away like a coon dog with a stolen slab of bacon when he heard Andy launch into his spiel again.

"Now, I can't guarantee I'll grab that first-place prize," Andy would tell anybody he could get to listen, "but there's big money for the top ten runners, and I know I can be in that bunch. I feel it in my bones! My feet, too! You can double your investment and help me bring glory to the Sooner State of Oklahoma at the same time!"

He approached the Claremore Chamber of Commerce, where he reminded them of all the races he won in high school. He had been an unbeatable miler. He had brought home first-place medals from state meets in Norman and Oklahoma City both. Why, he even outraced horses from time to time. Surely they remembered that!

"This is gonna be the biggest sports event of the entire year," he pleaded, "maybe the biggest one of the century! There'll be runners from every state in the union, maybe even from across the ocean. Red Grange himself's gonna trigger the starting gun! That proves it's legit!"

The fact that football legend Harold "Red" Grange, "The Galloping Ghost of Illinois," was a partner in sponsoring the race did grab people's attention. Grange was about the most famous sports hero in America, but most of the locals didn't think much of the other guy involved in the planning, C. C. ("Cash and Carry") Pyle. Oh, they'd read where Pyle called himself "The P. T. Barnum of Sports." But that just reminded them of Barnum's motto, "There's a sucker born every minute." Folks in Oklahoma were not going to be suckered into plunking down hard-earned cash on something as iffy as a footrace. No, sir, not in times as tough as these.

Even being told the race would be run right through their own towns didn't convince the citizens and merchants of Claremore and Foyil they should donate to Andy's cause. He assured them he'd be willing to work for the money, but they pointed out there was no way he could earn that much by March. As the days slipped by toward Christmas of 1927, Andy began to realize that this race had turned out to be between him and the clock, and it looked like the clock was going to win.

After another fruitless day of begging, Andy was jogging the five miles back to the farm when he decided there was nothing left to do but dig a big hole and stuff his dream of winning the First Annual International Trans-Continental Foot Race down in it. No use spoiling everybody else's Christmas by acting all broke up about it. He'd go back to looking for a regular job in Oklahoma and never mention that race to Vivian or his folks again.

But Andy's father had other ideas. In spite of the fact his farm was mortgaged, Mr. Payne patched together all the hope and courage he owned and took out a loan at the bank. A loan to cover the entry fee and the deposit on Andy Payne's dream. Mr. Andrew Lane Jackson Payne, whose friends called him "Doc," had never spent a day in a medical school, but he knew what was ailing Andy. That bank note, which gave Doc one hundred twenty-five dollars, might be just the prescription his son needed to cure his itchy feet.

Andy couldn't believe his eyes when he got home that cold December day and saw his smiling parents standing next to a stack of money on his mother's kitchen table. He reached out and touched it. He wasn't dreaming anymore. The money was really there. And it was his.

His folks believed he could win!

Andy packed for California again. This time he had the money for the race in his pocket and the will to win in his heart.

Chapter 4

Wings on His Feet

By January of 1928, Andy Payne was in California and running like his britches were on fire. The first time he read about the race, he had set his mind on winning. He knew a good endurance runner had to work his mind as hard as his feet and legs. Had to tell himself over and over to keep on going, keep on going. By the time he got to the end of that newspaper ad, Andy's brain had been ready to listen. Now he needed to get his body ready to run. Run like that Greek god Mercury he'd seen pictured in his ancient-history book. Mercury had wings on his hat and his feet. One of the gold medals Andy had won pictured an engraved foot with wings on the heel. He'd grow wings on his feet, too, if that was what it took to win that race.

Only two months remained between him and the March 4 starting date. He'd heard people say, "If March roars in like a lion, she'll frolic out like a lamb." He made up his mind that when the starting day arrived, no matter what mood March was in, he was going to be ready to roar.

He trained every day and dreamed every night. He sprinted up and down every Southern California street and hill and highway he could find to slap his shoe soles on. He was careful about what he ate and drank and got as much rest as he could between the odd jobs he took for room and board. Finally, he read in the paper that the Official International Trans-Continental Training Camp was ready to open in the oval of the Ascot Speedway. Andy Payne set off to meet his competition.

When he arrived at Ascot that rainy February 12, Andy was pretty sure he'd taken a wrong turn and accidentally stumbled into the California State Fair or a Hollywood movie set. The first guy he saw was dressed up like a character out of the Bible: Moses, maybe, or one of the disciples. He had hair clear down to his shoulders and a beard all the way down to his waist. The man next to him was strutting around in his underwear, and the boy behind him was playing a ukulele for his two hound dogs, who were wallowing around in the mud at his feet. Next to the hounds was a guy tying his running shoes with one hand because he only had one arm.

The program somebody shoved in Andy's hand listed more than two hundred men and boys ages sixteen to sixty-three signed up already, and more were standing in line to register. As he scanned the list, he discovered that the pot of gold at the end of this rainbow had drawn professional runners from as far away as Scotland, Germany, Finland, Ireland, Canada, Sweden, England, Greece, Turkey, Siberia, Italy, Australia, Poland, South Africa, Denmark, Switzerland, and Hungary! No wonder the talk around there sounded so strange. A lot of these people didn't even speak English!

The chatter and clatter in all those languages, along with the man dressed like Moses, brought to mind a story Andy's Sunday school teacher told him once. The tale about the Tower of Babel. None of the people in that tower could understand what anybody else was saying, and Andy sure as heck didn't understand what all was going on here. But he was mighty glad he was going to get to be part of it.

The first week, Andy found out that Peter Gavuzzi (from Italy by way of England) wore long underwear all the time, even when it was hotter than the back burner on a farmhouse cook stove. Gavuzzi had a beard as long as Lucien Frost's (the man who dressed like Moses), except his beard looked like a bird nested in it, and Lucien's was usually neat and trimmed. Andy knew any extra weight or trappings would take seconds off a person's stride, so he kept both his hair and his pants on the short side and shook his head every time he spotted Pete or Lucien running around with beards and wearing all those heavy clothes. He shook his head for a different reason when he saw the guys who were *walking* the practice track instead of running it.

Andy'd heard people talk about "run-walkers," but until he got to Ascot, he'd never seen one in person. Those crazy men had it in their heads that the fellows who walked fast and steady could outlast the runners in a marathon because they wouldn't wear themselves out. Andy had wondered how long it was going to take them to run almost three thousand five hundred miles; the thought of walking it boggled his mind. Those run-walkers had to be loco.

Andy quickly figured out which of the contestants were his competition and which had entered the race for fun. When he read the biographies on the program, he saw that a lot of the men held so many world records there wasn't room to list them all. He kept a sharp eye on the *real* runners so he could learn their tricks.

He knew from experience that clean, dry socks and sturdy shoes were the most important items a runner could own. He tended his meager supply every night and used every bit of money he could get his hands on to buy extra footgear for the weeks ahead. He chose high-top shoes to help protect his ankles. "You won't believe this," he wrote Vivian, "but some of these yokels run their training laps in Indian moccasins or lumberjack boots! They'll have bunions big as hens' eggs before we're off the starting blocks. In fact, the newspaper guys have already nicknamed this race 'The Bunion Derby'! Sure hope I don't grow me one of those!"

Even though the world's best runners were entered, Andy noticed that the reporters seemed more interested in people who could spin stories than they were in the ones who might actually win the race. But that was okay with him. Let those high-falutin' reporters crowd around the old man who walked with a cane or the champion swimmer from Florida who'd never raced on land in his life. Let them interview the guy who loved to tell how he skipped rope eleven thousand times in the same spot but had never run a single footrace. When this marathon was over, maybe those reporters would line up to interview Andy Payne from Oklahoma, who couldn't do anything but run.

Andy considered the "training" in the camp pretty loose, since every runner had his own ideas about what it took to get ready for the race and there was nobody around to tell them any different. Some of the men slept right through the six o'-clock wake-up call every morning, but Andy popped up from his iron bed like a jack-in-the-box clown. He ate breakfast and headed for the track, where he ran until he couldn't run any-more. He ran that oval so many times he lost track of the miles he was clocking ... twenty-five ... fifty ... some days more. He sure didn't plan to lose because his legs let him down.

He even picked himself up a trainer, a guy named Tom

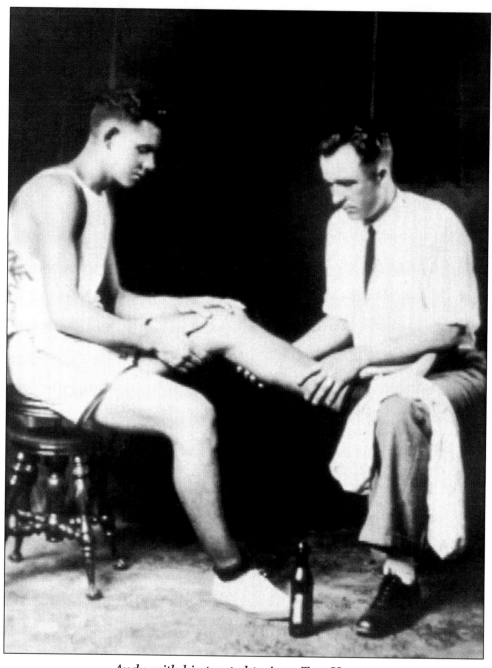

Andy with his trusted trainer, Tom Young.
—Vivian Payne collection

20

Young, who had come to the camp to enter the race but changed his mind when he saw how tough it was going to be. Tom rode a motorcycle, so when the race got started, he could run errands and bring water and snacks right up to where Andy needed them. Tom was an all-right guy who was willing to work for ten percent of the winnings, and Andy felt lucky to find him.

When his head hit the pillow each night, Andy tried to imagine how he would feel if he could run into New York City at the head of the pack. Mr. C. C. Pyle saw to it that news about his First Annual International Trans-Continental Foot Race made the front page of papers all over the world. Old "Corn and Callous" (as one paper called him) even had a portable radio-broadcasting station to travel with them. That station was so fancy and modern it could be heard for three hundred miles from wherever it was transmitting!

Mr. Pyle visited the camp almost every day and told the runners how grand the race was going to be, the grandest, most exciting, most wonderful sporting event ever held in the entire world, bigger than even the Olympics because those people in the Olympics just ran for gold medals.

In Mr. C. C. Pyle's First International Trans-Continental Foot Race, the contestants were running for the gold itself!

Chapter 5

Nature's Soft Nurse

Andy was hoping he'd get to use the same iron bed, the same soft pillow, and the same warm blanket he had in training camp during the race itself. Once he'd gotten used to the lumps and bumps, that gear had him sleeping like a hibernating bear. Sleep kept a person healthy, he told himself every night when he crawled under the covers earlier than everybody else. One sure-fire way to lose this race was to get sick.

"O gentle sleep! Nature's soft nurse ..." he whispered to his pillow as he pulled the blanket over his shoulders and settled in on the last night before the race was to begin. Now, where had those fancy words come from? Oh, yes, senior English class. The teacher made every last student memorize twenty-five lines from Shakespeare. Funny how something like that popped into a person's brain from time to time. ". . . sleep! Nature's . . . nurse . . ." Those were the only words he could remember, but they were enough to comfort him. He sure hoped nature was the *only* nurse he'd need during this race. He pulled the blanket tighter and patted his pillow like it was Blue Boy, his old hunting hound.

Just thinking about having to keep up with all those blankets and pillows, all those beds and boxes, all the trappings needed by as many people as there were in Mr. C. C. Pyle's traveling road race made Andy's head swim. He'd counted twenty different vehicles lined up to carry the people, the mess tent, and the portable hospital, as well as the carnival and sideshow. Mr. Pyle and Red Grange were going to ride in a big fancy bus, the same one that would carry the newspaper reporters, timekeepers, and other officials. Those people would get to roll down the road in style, but the runners were warned time and again that the only transportation they could use was attached to their ankles.

As Andy drifted off to sleep, the sounds of people packing up echoed through the cavernous tent. He was sure glad the only thing he had to worry about was running. Andy Payne was ready to let the world know why folks from Oklahoma were nicknamed "Sooners."

Publicity photo of C. C. Pyle's custom coach from the official race program.
                                    —Vivian Payne collection

25

Chapter 6

The Twice-as-Fast Runner

As Andy pulled his jersey over his head that March morning, he looked at his number, forty-three, and tried to figure some way to make it lucky. If he added the four and the three together, that made seven, and everybody knew seven was a lucky number. Or take the three away from the four and that left one. Number one! First place! Oh, yes! Forty-three was one lucky number for sure!

Right after the first of the year, a man Andy met delivering papers had informed him that 1928 was going to be a tough year for superstitious people.

"Has *three* Fridays on the thirteenth!" the guy informed him. "One in January, one in April, and one in July. Three

Fridays the thirteenth in those three months haven't happened since 1888! Won't happen again until 1956!" The guy, who claimed he was a genuine, certified mathematician, knew a ton of crazy number facts like that, and Andy admired him for it. Vivian had been a math major in college, so he wrote her all about it. Even though he wasn't superstitious himself, Andy knew the person who won this race was bound to need some luck along the way.

That first Friday the thirteenth, the one in January, slipped right by without him even noticing. No bad luck there. He checked the race schedule and figured out he'd be right in the middle of Oklahoma for the one in April. Couldn't anything bad happen to him in Oklahoma. And by the time July thirteenth rolled around, he would be so darned rich he wouldn't have to worry about luck anymore.

Yep, it might take some luck to come in first, but Andy knew the winner would not be the luckiest one. He would be the fastest one. Twice as fast as some of those guys, in fact. Yes, sir, that was what he intended to be: the twice-as-fast runner! Those words came from something else he'd had to memorize in school, but he couldn't think what it was. He checked his socks, pulled on his shoes, laced them up tight, and double knotted them. Couldn't depend on luck to keep your socks clean or your laces tied.

The opening race was not scheduled to start until three-thirty, because Mr. Pyle wanted to give the crowd plenty of time to gather. By the time Andy and the other runners approached the starting line, thousands of cheering fans had packed the Ascot Speedway and lined the streets to see them off. The first laps were to be taken around the racetrack itself. Then they'd go out the gate and on to Puente, California, sixteen miles away.

Andy could feel the blood pounding in his ears and the air filling his lungs from the bottom up as he took his starter's stance. He watched Red Grange, the fastest runner in college football, prepare to light the firecracker "bomb" that would signal the beginning of the number-one lap in the First Annual International Trans-Continental Foot Race across America. Somebody said that bomb was so big and loud it would rattle windows in San Diego.

The moment finally arrived.

The bomb went off.

The windows rattled.

And Andy Payne began to run.

Chapter 7

Sob-Story Pictures

Andy pasted a big old grin on his face and tried not to let his disappointment show when he looked up at the scoreboard in Puente that night. He hadn't even been fast enough to win the shortest lap of the race! He wasn't even in the top three! Everybody was clapping those three guys on the back, telling them what great legs they had. Well, at least they were runners, *real* runners, not some of that crazy, lumberjack-booted, banjo-playing bunch who'd signed up just to get their pictures in the paper.

Besides, two of those three at the top of the chart were listed in the program as being from New York City. Those guys probably burned up all their energy straight out of the chute since they knew the finish line was in their own hometown. Sure, that was it! He'd move to the top of the heap himself before long, before they reached the Oklahoma border for sure.

He smiled for real when he spotted Cotton Josephs, the only kid around younger than he was, coming in to check the boards, too. Sixteen-year-old Cotton, who was black, had kept a very straight face when he'd explained to Andy that he was named for a famous preacher and not that stuff you pick.

"Sure am glad they named me Cotton instead of 'Whitey,'" Cotton whispered before he broke up laughing at his own joke. Cotton's father was so sure his son was going to win, he had borrowed fifty dollars to buy a car so he could follow the race and cheer him on. Andy felt a special kinship with this kid whose father believed in him. When Cotton told him his younger brother had to drive because their father was paralyzed from the waist down, Andy got a lump in his throat. Cotton's family needed that money even more than his folks did!

"Beat you to that fence post," Cotton challenged, pointing out the open tent flap and taking off at the same time. Andy gave chase, but not with much vim and vigor.

Cotton won by a mile. Andy knew better than to use up good energy chasing a fence post! He lectured the kid about such foolishness but then promised to race him to the showers right after supper. Andy planned to be the first person in bed that night. He felt bad that Cotton wasn't allowed to sleep in his tent because of the color of his skin, but the black runners weren't the only ones who were segregated. Each ethnic group—Scandinavian, Indian, Mexican, French, and German—had a separate tent.

Instead of his sturdy iron bed, Andy found a rickety old cot waiting for him. He did have his same blanket, though. At least it looked like the same one. It had the same numbers on it, anyway. So did his pillow. He looked around at all those saggy old cots in the drafty, noisy tent and decided that the nights on this cross-country adventure were going to be just as long and uncomfortable as the days.

"Sleep . . . Nature's soft nurse . . ." he whispered again as he climbed onto his hard, drafty cot. The way he saw it, Nature might need to get herself a feather bed before this race was over.

Andy didn't need to wash anything but his feet at the end of the second day's lap. The clouds had taken turns wringing each other out until the runners sloshed along in mud up to their ankles. Andy'd heard that a racehorse was called a "mudder" if it did well on a wet track. He decided he was a "mudder" himself when he saw he'd zipped up twenty notches in the standings. Running to school and back in Oklahoma deluges year after year had prepared him for a day like this one. Andy Payne wasn't any wimpy little sugar cube that would dissolve in the rain!

That old sky juice did do away with some of the showoffs, though. Melted them right down into muddy puddles. When the first wave of wet, weary men dried their blistered feet and packed their bags to go home, Andy offered to help, but he couldn't think of anything to say to cheer them up. Now he understood why C. C. Pyle had insisted on that one-hundred-dollar deposit. Mr. *Pyle* planned to make a *pile* of money off this race. He had stated that fact right up front. He sure couldn't make money buying train tickets home for quitters, not if he had to pay for those tickets out of his own pocket. He'd already furnished those freeloaders room and board for over a month, he told them in no uncertain terms as they packed. He handed them their deposits, checked their names off the list, and didn't look the least bit sorry to see them go.

The Cajon Pass, that up-and-down, in-and-out, over-and-under Cajon Pass, chiseled the remaining ragtag runners away from the real ones in a hurry. That shin-splint-giving, stone-bruise-making slash in the earth had the photographers scrambling for a spot to shoot their sob-story pictures. They focused their cameras on blistered toes and sprained ankles of run-crippled men and snapped until they ran out of film. The pictures that appeared on the front pages of newspapers in the following days showed the world exactly how tough this Trans-Continental Foot Race was getting to be.

Andy didn't have to buy a paper to know that. He'd seen those people in person. They were still hobbling into the tent long after he had climbed into his bed. Some were even on crutches! Early on, Andy tried to keep track of the dropouts, but before long they were thicker than bees on a honeycomb, so he stopped counting.

Andy himself had cleared the Cajon with sweat stinging his eyes and nose, and aches rolling over his body from head to feet, but when he hit the sunshine at the bottom of the pass he was going full tilt. Before supper, the scorekeeper added up the times and announced that Andy Payne had run all the way up the chart to third place! He waited until he climbed into bed to start grinning, but he didn't stop then, not even when he went to sleep.

The men ahead of him were two of the professional runners he'd figured from the start were his strongest competition. The first was Ed "The Sheik" Gardner, from Seattle, who'd set all kinds of records in his home state of Washington. Ed was easy to keep track of since he always tied a bright red bandanna around his head. The other man was harder to spot because he ran without a single bounce and was always so far ahead.

Arthur Newton was a world champion who held every amateur running record Andy'd ever heard of and lots he hadn't. Newton had opted out of the Olympic games because he said the twenty-six-mile marathon was too short for him. He was an endurance runner who didn't hit his stride until after fifty, he told the press. Andy knew those two guys were going to be as hard to catch as greased lighting.

The next day, Andy wished for lightning, greased or otherwise. Or any other trick nature could toss at him to help take his mind off the heat—the searing, scalding, blinding heat of the Mojave Desert, which stretched in front of him in one big, long, shimmering wave. The wind grabbed up sand by the handful and rubbed it in his ears and eyes. He tried to pull his shirt up over his face, tried to run with his eyes shut, tried to imagine himself skinny-dipping in a big old farm pond. The sun beat down on him like a mallet on a powwow drum, steady and strong, and tried to melt him into the sand. But picturing the look on his folks' faces when he handed them the prize money helped him shake off the heat like a hosed-down hound dog and keep on running.

By the time they left California and streaked into Arizona, Andy could see Ed Gardner's red headband flapping in the wind like his own mama's hand waving him in from the field for supper. By Peach Springs, Andy passed Gardner and settled into second place. For the first time since the race began, his name was splattered in headlines across the country, and the announcers on that portable radio station were talking about him day and night. At last the newspaper reporters wanted to know everything there was to know about Andy Payne, the part-Cherokee Oklahoma farm boy who had never before won anything but high school track meets.

The only runner ahead of him now was Arthur Newton, but that didn't surprise anybody, least of all Andy. Newton was the best, the top favorite from the very first day. "Newton's Unbeatable!" several papers declared before the race had even started. "First Place Will Go to Newton!" others echoed. Andy had read those papers. So had everybody else. Nope, not one person in that race was surprised that Arthur Newton was in the lead. But what happened next surprised the whole world.

As the First Annual International Trans-Continental Foot Race neared Winslow, Arizona, after less than two weeks on the road, the unsinkable Arthur Newton of South Africa by way of England hit an iceberg and went down like the *Titanic*. To the amazement of every man, woman, and child who read about it—and Andy Payne, who heard about it firsthand—Arthur Newton announced he was quitting the race! His forty-four-year-old legs had given out, and his feet couldn't take another lap.

Andy Payne, the pride of Oklahoma, jumped right up into first place! There sure wasn't anything at all wrong with Andy's twenty-year-old feet and legs.

But he couldn't say the same for his throat.

In fact, just as he was leading the pack at last, Andy woke up to discover he couldn't say anything. His throat hurt him so bad he could barely swallow. He didn't think he could even get out of bed, much less run the next day's lap. He was certain that breathing the alkali dust in that dry desert air had seared his throat, but he sure as heck hadn't been able to run without breathing. He rubbed his neck with one hand and pounded his fist on the mattress with the other as he waited for Tom Young, his trainer, to come see why he wasn't getting out of bed.

Action photo of Andy during the race. Police escorts were often needed in the cities on the route.

—Vivian Payne collection

Chapter 8

Don't Tell 'Em

Andy couldn't remember ever feeling so rotten, but he knew he had to climb off that saggy old cot and run. He just had to. His folks were counting on him. Vivian was counting on him. His brothers and sister were counting on him. The entire state of Oklahoma was counting on him!

He begged Tom to keep the reporters away, pulled the blanket over his head, and slid as far down in the bed as he could slide. He knew bad news traveled fast, and if he didn't crawl out pretty soon, every danged reporter in that camp would be crowding around wanting to take his temperature!

He had to get up.

Had to put on his running jersey.

He just had to. He squeezed his eyes shut tight and tried his best not to swallow. Since he was usually one of the first at the breakfast table, some nosy news hound was bound to wonder where he was, especially since he had moved into first place. He wished for the good old days when none of those reporters even knew his name. The getting-up noises were starting all around him, and time was short. He'd promised Tom he would be at the starting line when everybody else was.

Andy sighed the biggest sigh of his life and dragged himself out of bed. He was so late he was the only one left in the tent. He pulled on his socks and shorts, shoved his feet into his shoes, and slid his jersey over his head. He tried to look down at his number, but it hurt too bad to bend his neck, so he just closed his eyes and traced the four and the three with his fingers. Then he sneaked over to the portable hospital.

"Tonsillitis," the doctor said, shaking his head as he pressed Andy's tongue with a wooden paddle and peered down his throat with a flashlight. "Bad case, too. Red as a Coca-Cola sign down there, son. Ought not to run today, but I'm sure you will. I'll give you something to take for it, but you're gonna have a hard time swallowing it. Sure am sorry. Especially since you're in the lead now."

"Don't tell the reporters, Doc," Andy begged him. "Please don't tell 'em."

"I won't have to tell 'em, son. They'll know when they see you try to run. But I'll tell them what I'll tell you. You're young. That's on your side. You're young and in good shape otherwise, so don't count yourself out. Minute your lap's done, you crawl into bed and stay there till it's time to run the next one. Sleep's the best medicine made." He patted Andy on the shoulder, shook his hand, and handed him a bottle of pills.

Sleep . . . Nature's soft nurse. He'd give half of any prize money he had coming if he could just go crawl back in that bed and let nature nurse him all day. But it was Tom, not nature, who was waiting outside the hospital tent with water and a little food. Andy's throat hurt so bad he couldn't swallow the biscuit.

"Got to at least get the water down," Tom whispered. "It'll help cool the fever. Sweatin' will do the same thing, if you got the energy to sweat. Told the reporters you were just a little 'off your feed.' Said the surprise of hearing about Newton dropping out, finding yourself in the lead, took some of the starch out of you, you being a kid and all. Right now they're all so busy trying to talk to Newton, you might gain a little time before they figure out how sick you are."

Andy knew if he could just stay on his feet and moving, the reporters would let him be until he finished the day's lap. Then he'd sneak back into bed before they could nab him. Pretend he was asleep. He sure didn't want his folks reading he was sick until he was feeling better. His mother, who hadn't wanted him to enter in the first place, and Vivian, who said she'd love him no matter who won, would worry themselves into a tizzy.

Tom could hop on that motorcycle and see to it that Andy had his medicine, along with water to wash it down. Tom was a better nurse than Nature, who had evidently ducked out during the night with Andy's good luck in her pocket.

Andy couldn't run a lick that day, but he did manage to walk the lap. He was so weak he had to lie down by the side of the road a couple of times to rest. By the time he staggered into the control station in the late afternoon, he had fallen three whole hours behind the new leader. He was tired as a hound at the end of a coyote hunt, and there wasn't a muscle in his body that didn't ache. But he had done what he'd set out to do. He'd finished the lap and kept from having to drop out of the race.

Andy shuffled off to his cot without telling Tom or anybody else good night. Even though it was a warm day, he was shivering from the fever. He closed his eyes and pretended he was back in his own bed in his own house with his mother piling all the covers she had on top of him.

"Want another blanket?" he heard a voice whisper right next to his ear. Andy popped his eyes open and saw Cotton kneeling next to the bed. "Don't sit up. Those snoopy reporters been looking for you high and low. I saw you sneakin' in here but don't think any of them did. Saw you by the side of the road today, too, Andy, but I just couldn't stop. I still got me a bit of a chance for some money, so I had to keep on runnin'. But I sure felt bad for you."

Talking was so painful Andy just nodded his head and tried to smile. Cotton spread his own blanket over his sick friend, tucked it in tight at both sides and the bottom, and sneaked out. Andy was asleep before the tent flap dropped shut.

Bunion Derby ID card.
—Vivian Payne collection

Chapter 9

Unexpected Pleasures

Andy had three long days of holding back before he was well again. That left him with a bushel basket full of time to make up. The newspaper reports didn't help his spirits any, either. The day Newton dropped out, the reporters had bombarded Andy with questions about what he was going to buy with his twenty-five-thousand-dollar first-prize money. But the minute they heard he was sick, they immediately declared that Andy Payne was done for. Finished. Out of the running. He decided those paper guys liked nothing better than taking the truth and standing it on its head, so he avoided them whenever he could. The heavy talkers who were now in the lead could give them all the quotes they needed. He'd go back to letting his feet do the talking.

Andy pounded the pavement like he was stomping red ants. Playing catch-up made him even more determined than when he was in the lead, and having to watch Ed Gardner's red bandanna flapping in the breeze in front of him again made him mad. Mad as one of those bulls in Mexico when he sees the matador's red cape. Gardner was so sure of himself he would stop to entertain the onlookers along the way or take a little rest in the shade of a nearby tree while Andy gritted his teeth and pumped his legs like out-of-control jackhammers.

When he finally swept past Seattle's pride a few days later, Andy grabbed that red bandanna off Ed's head like it was the prize in a game of "capture the flag." Gardner laughed so hard he had to stop and sit down to catch his breath. He was shaking his head and grinning when Andy made a big U-turn and ran back to toss the handkerchief in his friend's lap before he sprinted off again. Getting the lead back was important, but so was friendship.

Crossing the Continental Divide got the American runners as excited as the foreigners. Everybody had heard about that awesome mountain range, the place in New Mexico where water runs in two different directions, but they never expected their very own feet to touch down on that spot!

After the divide came a detour off of Route 66 with only cardboard arrows marking the trail through miles and miles of sagebrush. Mr. Pyle had made another crazy financial deal, which included changing the route, and as usual the runners were the ones who had to pay the price. Before long they were all making bets on what "unexpected pleasures," as Ed called them, would come next on this seemingly never-ending journey.

What came was a rebellion, a small mutiny in fact, and Andy was glad when it happened. In fact, he thought it was long overdue, but he was not a person who went looking for trouble. That was one place he'd gladly let the others take the lead.

C. C. Pyle had what Andy's father called a golden tongue. Most of the time when something went wrong—and there were lots of things to go wrong in an event as long and complicated as the First Annual International Trans-Continental Foot Race—Pyle could talk his way out of the corners he had painted himself into. But this night the runners were tired and their stomachs were empty. Even a person with a golden tongue knows better than to argue with hungry men.

"No more stew!" one of the Finns hollered when Pyle marched into the protest meeting the runners had organized. "Ten days in a row is nine more than we need! We need stick-to-the ribs food served on clean dishes, not on plates and cups wiped off with a dirty towel!"

"And water with every meal! Lots of water!" another demanded.

"You're right! You're absolutely right!" Pyle interrupted before the angry crowd could gather more steam. "And I don't blame you for being mad! Don't blame you at all!" He shifted his voice into a soft, soothing gear. "I promise we'll get you better food. Arrange for you to sleep in hotels and rooming houses as soon as we get to places where such things are available. Hard to provide all you deserve way out here in the middle of Texas. Why, we're over a hundred miles from civilization right now. But we'll be back in the real world before very long. You fellows hold on, now! You're a sturdy lot! Won't be long!"

They were too tired to put up much of a fight, so after a few more demands were voiced, they grumbled their way to the supper line. Ed Gardner, who among other roles liked to play ringmaster in Pyle's circus-like tent, broke the tension by suggesting that the men who had moved into the top three spots should be allowed to lead them in to supper.

With a big bow and a pantomimed drum roll, "The Sheik" Gardner announced, "Gentlemen and gentlemen! I give you Mr. Peter Gavuzzi of England, Dr. Arne Souminen, of Detroit, Michigan, by way of Finland, and Mr. Andrew Payne, of Oklahoma, a state our happy feet will soon get to greet!" Everybody applauded and gave the three men, as well as the ringmaster, a big cheer. They didn't like Pyle much, but they sure did like one another.

Almost one-third of the race had been run, and Andy was back on top. But the weather was about to give every single one of them a punch in the jaw that would have sent even Gene Tunney, heavyweight boxing champion of the world, reeling to the mat.

Chapter 10

Favorite Son

The runners from across the ocean—England, Ireland, Italy, places like that—had never heard the term "blue norther" in their lives. Andy Payne from Oklahoma knew exactly what a blue norther was. Blue was the color his skin turned when he had to go out to feed and water the cows with the arctic air swooshing down from the north and snapping the thermometers right off the fence posts.

"A body brave enough to stand out in a blue norther can actually watch that silver mercury slide down the tube before it busts!" Andy informed the shivering foreigners who gathered around him for a weather report. "Why, I've seen it drop twenty degrees in one hour. I'd advise you to try to buy some of that long underwear off of Lucien or Pete. They got extras, I bet. Miserable night ahead of us, and even more miserable day tomorrow."

Andy was right. Sifting, shiver-selling snow swirled around their tents the next morning. They peeked out from under their thin, worn blankets and put off getting up as long as they could.

"Don't know about you guys," Andy grumbled as they dressed for the next lap, "but I'm not waiting for runnin' to warm my blood this day. Don't give a fig if extra weight does cut my time. Time won't matter anyhow if I'm dead of pneumonia!" He piled on every sweater and shirt in his suitcase, pulled his rain slicker over his head, and headed for the starting line. Their next destination was Amarillo, Texas.

Mike Joyce, the jolly Irishman from Cleveland, Ohio, lined up next to Andy like he did most days. Mike was thirty-four and an old-timer at marathon running. The two of them were among the few who made the Mojave Desert crossing without a single blister or shin splint, and that had drawn them closer. Andy knew he had a lot to learn from Mike, and he got a kick out of imitating his Irish brogue.

"I'm gonna imagine this norther of yours is green instead of blue," Mike informed Andy as they stood at the starting line, slapping their hands and stomping their feet to get the blood circulating. "Warm color, green, 'specially if 'tis Kelly's shade. If I could but capture me a wee leprechaun, I could pull his beard till he turned the snow green as grass! That'd get me Irish up!"

"Sure'n you're full to the brim of blarney, Michael me lad, but I'll stop and peek under every toadstool we pass," Andy said, laughing. "In the West Texas sand, that won't take much off me time! Chances are, if we did capture us a wee one, Mr. Pyle'd stick the little fellow in the carnival before he could holler, 'St. Patrick, preserve me!' 'Tis said by many that the only green old Cash and Carry knows about is the kind that fits in his billfold!"

Old Cash and Carry, who kept them all on edge wrangling about money in every town they went through, proved Andy right that very night. Without any prior warning, he shut down the food and sleeping tents.

"Gonna give each and every one of you two dollars and fifty cents right out of my pocket every single day from now till the end of the race, rain, shine, or snow!" he said with a big grin as if he were doing them a wonderful favor. "Pickin' your own food'll be lots better than having me pick it for you! Same thing goes for the place you lay your head! You get to select that for yourself, too. Better for all of us! Lots better!"

Nobody was sure about that. Life in the tents was pretty miserable, but at least they always knew where to head after supper. Searching for food and a bed in a different town every night was going to be tough, but they were too cold and tired to argue. Besides, most of them were trying to warm their hands in empty pockets, so they grabbed Mr. Pyle's two-fifty and spread out over a surprised Amarillo populace. The people of the town had been expecting runners who streaked in and out, not boarders who also needed places to sleep.

Andy had figured out right away that runners with money, guys like Dr. Souminen from Detroit, or Harry Gunn, whose father followed along in a fancy Pierce Arrow automobile, had a big advantage over the poor folks like him and Cotton and Mike. Rich guys could buy decent food instead of eating slop, get a new pair of shoes whenever they needed them, and rent a nice hotel room instead of sleeping on saggy old cots.

Andy also noticed, however, that those same rich guys didn't ever seem to pace themselves, didn't take much note of the fact that this was an endurance contest as well as a footrace. Day after day those guys drained their energy tanks early and then needed help getting their shoes untied. When Dr. Souminen, one of the top ten, had to drop out because of a strained tendon not long before they reached the Oklahoma border, Andy was sorry. Sorry, but not surprised.

He did have a surprise coming, though. And it was a big one. A surprise that would boost him up into the same category as those fine-food-eating, good-bed-sleeping rich guys.

When the people of the Sooner State heard their "favorite son" was back in first place by over two hours in total time, they passed the hat and offered a one-thousand-dollar check to the first runner to cross the state line. There was no doubt at all who that first runner would be.

Andy Payne was about to run the next laps of the First Annual International Trans-Continental Foot Race on a red carpet! A red carpet rolled out all the way across the state of Oklahoma just for him! His feet had never had it so good.

And the rest of his body didn't have anything to complain about, either.

Chapter 11

Cherokee Kid

Doc Payne was so excited about Andy's first-place showing he couldn't stand to wait until his son reached the Oklahoma border to congratulate him. He jumped on a train and chugged across the state and over into Texas to greet Andy on Lone Star State soil. Mr. Pyle, seeing a chance for fresh publicity with a family angle, invited the proud father to join him in his fancy bus. The next day, when Andy leaped the invisible state line like it was a high hurdle, Mr. Andrew Lane Payne surprised his son by jumping out of the big fancy bus to greet him.

Andy stopped long enough to take the one-thousand-dollar check and hand it to his beaming father. They slapped each other on the back, hugged for the cameras, and watched the mob of well-wishers pile back in their cars to escort the now famous Mr. Andrew Hartley Payne across his home state.

For mile after mile, Oklahoma people lined the country roads as well as the small-town streets to cheer as Andy passed. Farmers left their tractors running in the field to gallop to the fences and wave their straw hats, and country schools canceled classes so the pupils and teachers could trot along next to the state's newest "Cherokee Kid." Will Rogers had owned that nickname for a long time, but now it was Andy's turn. In his daily newspaper column, Will complained that a young whippersnapper named Payne had stolen both of his nicknames ("Cherokee Kid" *and* "Favorite Son"), but he admitted he was more than happy to share to both titles. Members of the Cherokee tribe proudly claimed that the famous twosome were fine examples of what mixed blood could accomplish in the white man's world, and reporters quickly added their agreement.

Andy had figured he'd hit the state capital right around noon on the unlucky Friday the thirteenth in April, and he was right. The crowds of well-wishers had kept him from winning a single lap since he entered the Sooner State, but he was still ahead of the field in total elapsed time. The over one thousand horn-honking, exhaust-spewing cars that were following him by the time he reached Oklahoma City made every step a worry. He'd been so careful not to turn an ankle or get a stone bruise, it would be bad luck of the worst kind if one of those drivers leaned out the window to pat him on the back and ran him down instead!

Andy breathed a sigh of relief when the runners were diverted to a back road to the fairgrounds and the cars were not allowed to follow. The move made their day's lap a lot longer than it was supposed to be, but they'd learned early on that Mr. Pyle stretched the laps the same as he did the truth if he could make an extra buck in the process.

"Cash and Carry" Pyle saw the capital city as a big pond where he could cast his net and haul in a great big load of greenbacks. The profits he'd dreamed of reaping had been slipping through his fingers like water through a minnow bucket since the race left Arizona. The towns weren't coming through with the pledges they had promised, and all those runners he thought would drop out and quickly go home had still cost him room and board.

In spite of the fact it was Friday the thirteenth, Pyle figured his luck was about to change from bad to good. The Oklahoma City Chamber of Commerce had promised him five thousand dollars to divert the race through downtown, and his traveling sideshow, which had been paying for overhead expenses, would draw its largest crowds so far at the Oklahoma State Fair grounds. After all, the feature attraction was one of the Sooner State's most famous outlaws, Elmer McCurdy, a man who had actually been *dead* for seventeen years.

McCurdy, who never drew a second glance from anybody

in his short life of crime, pulled in long lines of gawkers every-where his opened coffin was propped. Churchgoing folks ob-jected from time to time, but C. C. Pyle noticed that those very same Christians were eager to stare at the bank robber's corpse and hear McCurdy's story. "The Sheik" Gardner had perfected a monologue wherein he pretended to be Elmer, telling the story of how he was shot to death in a hayloft near Pawhuska, Oklahoma; how his body had been embalmed and stuck in the window of the funeral home when nobody claimed it; how the combination of the hot west-window sun and an overdose of embalming fluid had petrified the body just like one of those Egyptian mummies. Right from the start, McCurdy had been their biggest draw.

Elmer, who had been dead since 1911, still looked so much like a live human being that one of the photographers snapped him and put the picture in the paper, claiming it was a Bunion Derby runner after he'd crossed the Mojave Desert! Mr. Pyle didn't deny it, either. After all, that kind of publicity sold tickets. But on that bad-luck Friday the thirteenth in Oklahoma City, the newspaper headlines about old Cash and Carry were not the kind he wanted to see.

A former baseball player who had also coached Pyle's New York Yankee team showed up at the big state house gathering and claimed the five-thousand-dollar check about to be handed Mr. Pyle was owed to him in back wages. The next day, an Oklahoma judge agreed, and radios and newspapers across the

"ANDY" PAYNE

EDITION OF THE
OFFICIAL PROGRAM

Andrew Payne crosses the Oklahoma state line ahead

C. C. PYLE'S

PRICE 10 CENTS

First Annual
International
Trans-Continental
Footrace

Andy became so popular in his home state that an official "Andy Payne" edition of the program was published for his fans.

—Vivian Payne collection

nation proclaimed C. C. Pyle a promoter who had to be forced by law to pay his debts.

As Andy and the other runners heard the news and read the papers, they began to do some serious worrying about the existence of the prize money for the First Annual International Trans-Continental Foot Race. Surely, they told each other over and over again, *surely* Mr. Pyle had it stashed away in a New York City bank. Surely he would not have let them suffer as they had suffered and then not be able to pay the winners. Andy pushed that thought as far back in his brain as it would go and kept right on running.

By the time the Tulsa skyline came into view, Bunion Derby fever in the Oil Capital of the World was as hot as the cement under the tired runners' blistered feet. Bus loads of bands drove in from all over eastern Oklahoma, and the excited high school students marched after the lead-off Claremore ensemble like the children who followed the Pied Piper. Several black communities, eagerly wanting to lend support to Ed Gardner, Cotton Josephs, and the other black runners, sent musical representatives, too. A carnival atmosphere roared through downtown Tulsa like an Oklahoma tornado.

Andy smiled for so many cameras, he was afraid he'd never be able to wipe the grin off his face. Not even if he lost. But he wasn't going to lose; he knew that now. Not unless he got sick again or got run over by one of those danged automobiles! He might not haul in the first-place prize, but he was sure to be in the top three. Second place got ten thousand dollars, and third was five thousand. Either of those slots would allow him to pay off the mortgage on the farm and buy some land of his own to live on when he and Vivian got married. But twenty-five thousand . . .

Twenty-five thousand dollars! If he could win that twenty-five-thousand-dollar prize, he'd be almost as rich as Andrew Carnegie! Andrew Carnegie was the richest person Andrew Payne had ever heard of, and the fact that they shared the same first name had made Andy take notice of Mr. Carnegie early on. Andrew Carnegie had given the money for hundreds of libraries to be built all over America and then put his name right up on the front of them. Collinsville, which was just up the road from Foyil, had a Carnegie Library. Andy'd seen it when they'd visited there, and he'd never forgotten how grand it was. Maybe Andrew Payne could build a library someday, too!

Andy got stopped and welcomed so many times, he lost the lead in elapsed time for a little while, but by the day he entered Claremore, he had caught up with and passed the long-underwear-wearing, second-place Pete Gavuzzi by a couple of hours. His Irish friend, Mike, was still in the top ten, and Andy was happy about that, but he hadn't had time to check on anybody else's placement on the board. He knew Cotton was falling farther behind every day, but Cotton was too proud to quit. Andy knew family pride would keep Cotton in the race until he had crossed the finish line.

Since the day he'd left Los Angeles, Andy had been doing a lot of dreaming about eating supper in his own house and spending time with Vivian, but he had a hard time slipping away from the crowd that packed downtown Claremore. Every kid in town wanted to get a look at him and get his autograph. A man from the Chamber of Commerce slipped a hundred-dollar note in his hand, and everybody he passed wanted to take his picture. It wasn't until the sun was going down that he was finally able to head for the farm and home.

His mother had fixed all his favorite foods, and of course Vivian had been invited to share in their celebration. Sitting at his parents' supper table, surrounded by all the people he loved and cared about, Andy wished more than once that the First Annual International Trans-Continental Foot Race across America was over and that he was home to stay. But that same schoolteacher who had him memorize Shakespeare had also taught him, "If wishes were horses, beggars might ride."

Wishing wasn't going to get him anywhere. But *running* would. The quicker the runners were on their way again, the sooner their ordeal would be

*This action photo of Andy taken in El Reno, Oklahoma,
was published in the state's largest newspaper.*
—Copyright the Oklahoma Publishing Company

over and they could claim their prize money. If the prize money was there to be claimed. But he wasn't going to think about that now. He was home with his family and Vivian, and he was happy.

Hard as it was to say good night, he hugged everybody and headed for bed early. This visit home was the spring tonic he needed to keep him well for the rest of the trip.

The next morning, with eighty runners still on their feet and Andy Payne still in the lead, the Bunioneers crawled out of their beds once more. By sunrise, they had taken off for the last half of their odyssey across America.

Chapter 12

The Iron Man

Andy liked Pete Gavuzzi, the man who was nipping at his heels in second place. Liked him a lot. The newspapers started calling the two of them "The Sister Act" because they always seemed to be running side by side. Andy joined the fun and started calling Pete his "sister."

"Got three more just like him back in Oklahoma," Andy joked in a radio interview one day. "Not one of them has a beard, though. Can't run as good as he can, either, but they're a whole lot prettier!" The friendship between Andy and Pete generated a lot of fun stories for the newspaper writers, who were always looking for fresh angles to keep their stories on the front page.

"When this race is over, you can come back to Oklahoma with me, and we'll polish up our act. Sing and dance our way to Broadway, Sister Pete. Why, we might even talk Will Rogers into joining us," Andy teased the little Italian as they jogged along together. "My father knew Will when they were kids. Used to break horses with him."

By peeking in the tent flaps, the reporters discovered that the "sisters" began most mornings studying the route together and trading ideas on how to save their energy and avoid injuries. Pete was only two years older than Andy, but he smoked and drank whiskey and ate spaghetti for breakfast. His long, flowing beard, Italian accent, and funny eating habits made him a much more interesting interview than the Indian stoic Andy. In fact, Andy was so quiet around the reporters they could hardly pull a quote out of his mouth.

As a joke, one of the reporters nicknamed the skinny, bandy-legged Pete "The Iron Man." When the cheering throngs along the route got a gander at the Iron Man in person, the puny little Pete began to draw a following of wild and crazy fans across the Midwest. He couldn't believe his ears when he ran down street after street lined with Americans who chanted his name and carried banners urging, "Run, Iron Man, Run!" In towns with Italian populations, he was mobbed for autographs and photographs, and he had expected that. But Americans wanting him to win? This country truly was the land of opportunity for all!

Pete responded to this surprising surge of encouragement from such a large number of total strangers by pounding the pavement harder and faster. Day after day, city after city, he left Andy behind to perform their "Sister Act" alone. By the time they reached Lincoln, Illinois, the Iron Man had lived up to his name and moved five whole hours ahead of Andy in total elapsed time! Pete Gavuzzi was beginning to look unbeatable, and Andy's father made up his mind to do something about it. Andrew Lane "Doc" Payne, age seventy, decided to enter the race himself.

Andy did his best to keep from laughing when his father lined up next to him and took a starter's stance. He knew Doc was trying to boost his sagging spirits, so he gave him a hug and warned Pete that now the real competition was about to begin. After jogging a mile or so down the road, Doc caught a ride with one of the delighted newspapermen, who got paid for his taxi service with a column full of quotes. The fun of the day, however, didn't cut Gavuzzi's lead. He was still five whole hours ahead.

The Iron Man decided to celebrate his big lead by jogging into a barbershop and having his long beard shaved off and his hair cut short. He had finally decided all that hair was weighing him down.

"You never heard that story about Samson in the Bible?" Andy teased when he saw Pete's baby pink, clean-shaven face and short hair for the first time. "Samson lost his strength

A billboard ad for the First Annual International Trans-Continental Footrace welcomes the Bunioneers to St. Louis, Missouri.

—Vivian Payne collection

when he let that woman clip his hair, remember? Been worried about you this past week or so, Pete, but I'm not gonna worry anymore! Won't be long now till your strength just slips away! You shoulda learned a lesson from the Bible and kept your hair!"

When Pete started slowing down a few days later, Andy stroked his friend's beardless chin, ruffled his newly shorn head, and reminded him again about Samson. When Pete's lead-time continued to shrink, Andy became really worried about his friend's health. He finally got Pete to confess that he was suffering from an abscessed tooth. Andy didn't know who felt worse, Pete or him. He got Pete to a doctor, but by that time the infection had moved into the Iron Man's bloodstream, and Pete was forced to drop out of the race. Andy moved back into first place again, but he wasn't in any mood to celebrate.

Pete took his loss of the prize money better than Andy did. Andy wanted to beat the scrappy little Italian fair and square, not because of a rotten tooth. Those doctors in that moveable hospital of theirs were always shaking their fingers at people who didn't take care of their feet, legs, and ankles. Now they'd have to add teeth to their checklist.

When the reporters asked Pete what he was going to do now that his racing days were over, he laughed and told them he was going to go look up Lucien Lee and recommend his barber to him. A few days earlier, Lucien, the Moses imitator, had been kicked out of the race for hitching a ride in the trunk of a car.

He'd been caught when he forgot to tuck in his beard and an eagle-eyed judge spied it flapping in the breeze as the vehicle pulled into town. Will Rogers had the world laughing when he wrote in his column that "Moses" had failed in his attempt to cross the "Red Sea," otherwise known as the Mighty Mississippi.

Andy wasn't laughing about all the dropouts, though. He was truly sorry to see the Sister Act broken up and Lucien kicked out, because both men had become his friends. But he had a race to win. New York City was still a long way off, and Pete's tooth troubles reminded Andy that the race could be over for any one of them in blink of an eye or the snip of a barber's scissors.

In the long days and nights that followed Indiana, where Pete's tooth had become abscessed, and Ohio, where he dropped out of the race, Andy still enjoyed the company of his Irish friend Mike Joyce. Mike was always bouncing around in the top five on the placement board, but "Mighty Mike," as the papers dubbed him, had never been a threat for the first-place spot. Mike's competition for the third through fifth slots was a couple of walkers-turned-runners.

Phillip Granville and Ginsto Umek had both shifted into a running gear when they realized that running was the only way they'd end up in the money. From the beginning, the walkers and the runners had been jawing back and forth like bluejays fighting over a worm, so Andy thoroughly enjoyed reminding them that running was the only way to win a footrace.

Postcard photo of Italian runner and fifth-place finisher Ginsto Umek, sent to Andy after race. The two remained friends for many years.
                                                    —Vivian Payne collection

Andy soon struck up a friendship with the man who moved into second place when Pete dropped out. Johnny Salo was from New Jersey, and for a little while after he'd moved up, he tried to challenge Andy for the top spot. However, when they were entering the final days and Johnny was still fifteen to twenty hours behind in total elapsed time, he announced that he would concede first place and settle for the second-place prize of ten thousand dollars.

"Andy's a better runner than I am," Johnny told the newspaper reporters who gathered around for his announcement. "I'm just proud to have been able to run with such a man."

That was one of several reasons Andy Payne couldn't believe his ears when one of those same reporters informed him there was a car in New Jersey waiting to run him down! And, the reporter continued as he gripped his pencil and got ready to write, to make matters worse, that car was being driven by friends of Johnny Salo!

Chapter 13

Good as Gold

Because crazy rumors had buzzed around the runners' tents since the first night of the race, Andy brushed this one off like a mule's tail swatting a horsefly. A car running him down on purpose? Driven by friends of Salo? Sounded to him like a newspaper hoping to run down some gullible customers.

Johnny Salo was a military veteran, a member of the American Legion. Salo had sewn Legion emblems and American flags onto every shirt he owned. The man had a wife and two little kids. He was always passing their pictures around. That kind of guy wouldn't try to win a race by getting his competition run over! Andy was certain of that.

But at breakfast the next morning, Mike recalled how many

times Johnny had told them his friends in the Finnish-American Athletic Club were totally convinced Johnny could win first prize. So convinced, in fact, they had talked Johnny into quitting his job in the ship yard to enter. Now this nice, patriotic man with a wife and two children to support didn't even have a job, Mike pointed out. Maybe Johnny's friends felt so guilty they had decided to help him out. Remove his only competition. The fifteen thousand dollars that separated the first- and second-place prize money might just have been too much of a temptation.

"Lots of folk in this wicked world'd do almost anything for fifteen thousand dollars, Andy me boy," Mike assured him between bites of bacon. Andy just shook his head and kept on chewing his toast, but the lump in his throat made it hard for him to swallow.

"I know for a fact Johnny wouldn't go along with anything underhanded, Mike," Andy stated firmly as they were stretching for the run into New Jersey. "Just can't believe he'd be a party to anything bad like that. That's gangster-movie stuff."

"He might not even know about it! You'd be a fool not to at least ask for police protection," Mike insisted. "The driver of that car might think he would do Johnny a favor and then try to squeeze him for a payoff later."

The people in the town of Passaic got madder than a gang of alley cats sprayed with a garden hose when they got wind of the rumors about Johnny Salo. They immediately sent their local politicians to reassure Andy and the other runners while they traced the rumor to the Associated Press, who, as Andy had guessed, simply wanted to sell more newspapers.

In the weeks since the race began, the Associated Press had carried detailed stories about the wild celebrations other places had thrown for their hometown runners. Passaic, New Jersey, decided to outdo all those other towns and at the same time keep a crazy, unfounded rumor from raining on their parade.

The Gerald V. Carroll Post of the American Legion announced that Andy Payne and Johnny Salo would both be their guests for the night in the town's finest hotel. The local commissioner of safety sent two motorcycle policemen to escort Andy for the entire time he ran in New Jersey and then onto the Forty-second Street Ferry, where the Bunioneers were to cross over into New York. Furthermore, Johnny Salo would be hired as a policeman for the city of Passaic at a salary of two thousand dollars a year! That, along with his ten-thousand-dollar second-place prize money, would make him a man who didn't need help from anybody.

When Andy heard the news, he breathed a sigh of relief. Now the only thing left to worry about was exactly when and where Mr. Pyle was going to hand him his prize money. Andy, the guy who had the most to lose, seemed to be among the few people left who felt sure the money would be paid.

Every day for weeks the newspapers had printed story after story about how broke Mr. "Cash and Cary" Pyle was, how the race had been a financial bust from start to finish, and how there wasn't going to be any payoff for the winners.

As the reporters sorted through the facts, it seemed there were two reasons Mr. Pyle had not been able to make the race pay the big money he'd expected it to generate. The first was the spirit of the runners, who just wouldn't quit. Before the race began, Pyle often stated he didn't think more than fifteen of the two-hundred-plus men would finish the race. The fifty-five who had stuck with it until the end had been a big drain on his finances, since he had fed and housed them for well over two months. He also blamed the towns that had promised they would pay him for an overnight stay and then couldn't come up with the money. As the race neared its end, he finally admitted publicly that the runners might not be paid right away. He stopped short of saying just how long they might have to wait.

"Mr. Pyle is good as gold," Andy assured one of the many newspaper reporters who was looking for a quote from him to keep the rumor pot boiling. Andy put both hands in his pockets so he could cross his fingers without them being seen and hoped with all his heart that he was right.

Chapter 14

Runner's Heart

As bad as Andy wanted to get the race over with and go back to Oklahoma, he understood why Johnny Salo hated to leave Passiac and head for New York City. When they entered Johnny's town, there had been a near riot among the city officials, who were all trying to be the first to shake his hand. They didn't care if Johnny had taken first place or not. He was their hero, and they planned to cheer him on right to the finish line. The next morning, it looked as if every person in town who owned a car had packed it with their friends and family and gotten ready to follow Johnny across the Forty-second Street Ferry and on to Madison Square Garden.

At first, the city-born New Yorkers, who were used to seeing strange sights every day of their lives, didn't pay much attention to the caravan of mud-caked vehicles that rumbled down the street behind the runners. Even the truck with the giant-sized coffee pot on the bed and the sign emblazoned "Coast to Coast" didn't stir up a lot of interest. But as word got around as to exactly who those runners were, thousands began to line the streets, and thousands more began running to Madison Square Garden to watch the entrance of the now world-famous Bunioneers.

Andy had a hard time not turning an ankle or bumping into something as he trotted along with his head thrown back and his chin in the air, drinking in the famous New York City sky-

The truck that served Maxwell House coffee to C. C. Pyle's marathon cross-country runners.
—MAXWELL HOUSE® is a registered trademark of KF Holdings

line for the first time. He did look down in time to get a glimpse of Cotton Josephs' father's old jalopy stalled on Eighth Avenue. Andy was turning around to go back and help when he saw Mr. Pyle stop taking in money in order to gather up some of the crew and command them to push the Josephs' car on down the street and into the Garden.

When Andy saw C. C. Pyle do that, when he heard that tight-fisted money grubber of a promoter explaining to the crew that it was very important for Mr. Josephs to be there at the end, for him to see his son finish what he had started, Andy decided old Cash and Carry did have a heart, after all. And that heart was located in his chest, not his billfold. Mr. Pyle would see to it that his runners got paid, because his heart was in the right place.

At that moment, the words "runner's heart" popped up in Andy's brain just like "sleep . . . Nature's soft nurse" and "twice-as-fast runner" had popped into his mind other times during the race. "Runner's heart," he whispered to himself as he tapped his chest and remembered.

Dr. Jesse Bushyhead had taught him about the "runner's heart" when Andy was still in grade school. Dr. Bushyhead was a very smart man. His father was principal chief of the Cherokee two times, and Dr. Jesse had taken care of the Payne family as long as Andy could remember. The kindly doctor was just leaving their farm one spring day when Andy dashed into the front yard from school. The doctor was well aware of

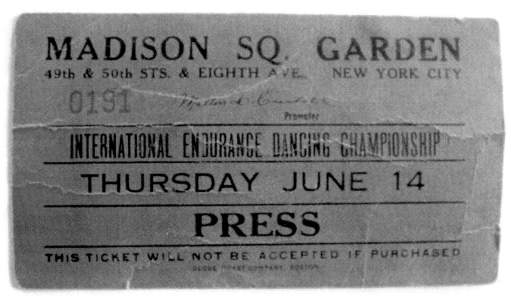

A Bunion Derby press pass allowing the holder entry into New York City's Madison Square Garden.

—Vivian Payne collection

Andy's love of running, so he had stopped long enough to give the boy a little free medical advice.

"Someday, when you're all grown up, some fancy doctor's probably going to tell you that all that running you've done has given you a 'runner's heart,' Andy my boy," he said, putting his bag down and propping his foot on his running board. "Now, 'runner's heart' means a ticker that gets bigger and bigger over the years, until sometimes it's just too danged big for a person's chest. A horse's heart can get that way, too, for that matter. From what I hear, you can outrun most horses, can't you? But you need to know they can have the same problem." He had smiled at Andy and mussed his hair before he went on.

"That same doctor might warn you that 'runner's heart' can make that old ticker of yours bust right open. And it does, sometimes it does. But I've always figured 'runner's heart' had another meaning, a more important meaning than doctors give it. All the runners I ever knew, *real* runners, won't ever quit, not until they cross that finish line at the end. That's the difference between runners and ordinary people. Lots of people give up when the going gets tough, when life gives them a stitch in their side, when they get a blister on their toe or their shins begin to hurt. But runners, runners never quit the race until it's over. Not even if they have to take every single one of those last laps all by themselves. That's the difference between runners and ordinary people. I'm certain that's what 'runner's heart' really means, and you ought to be mighty proud you got one."

Andy had rolled that talk around inside his head many times over the years. Now he knew for certain that Mr. C. C. Pyle had a runner's heart. And so did Cotton Josephs and the other forty-four men who kept on running that horribly long race until the very end, even though they didn't have a chance to win a single penny.

They had runner's hearts, every last one of those men who finished the First Annual International Trans-Continental Foot Race. And as Andy Payne entered Madison Square Garden in first place, he would have bet the farm, which would soon be his family's free and clear, he would never forget a single one of them.

Studio portrait of Andy Payne wearing his Bunion Derby number.
—Vivian Payne collection

Afterword

Old Cash and Carry lived up to his "run now, get paid later" nickname when on Friday, June 1, 1928, he awarded his runners partial payments and promissory notes for the rest. After giving them a few weeks more of anxious days and nights, he did eventually pay off everybody in full.

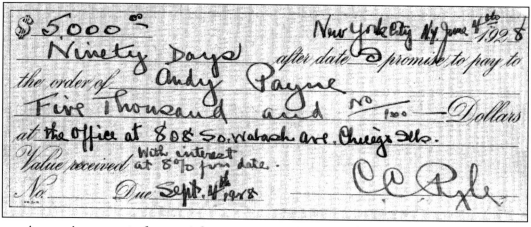

A promissory note for partial payment to winner Andy Payne from promoter C. C. Pyle.

—Vivian Payne collection

The amounts, names, and countries of the prize winners were as follows:

$25,000	1. Andy Payne, Foyil, Oklahoma, USA
$10,000	2. Johnny Salo, Passaic, New Jersey, USA
$5,000	3. Phillip Granville, Hamilton, Ontario, Canada
$2,500	4. Mike Joyce, Ireland
$1,000	5. Ginsto Umek, Triest, Italy
$1,000	6. William Kerr, Minneapolis, Minnesota, USA
$1,000	7. Louis Perella, Albany, New York, USA
$1,000	8. Ed "The Sheik" Gardner, Seattle, Washington, USA
$1,000	9. Frank R. Von Hue, Kerman, California, USA
$1,000	10. John Cronick, Saskatoon, Saskatchewan, Canada

Over ninety hours separated the first- and tenth-place winners in elapsed time, with Andy beating Johnny Salo by fifteen and a half hours. Andy gladly wrote out a check for two thousand five hundred dollars to his trainer, Tom Young, and allowed as to how it was the best money he ever spent.

Receipt of payment from Tom Young for services as trainer for Andy Payne during the race.
—Vivian Payne collection

Studio portrait of Andy Payne, winner of the famous 1928 Bunion Derby.
—Vivian Payne collection

Andy Ever After

After winning the Bunion Derby, Andy Payne went back to Oklahoma, paid off the family farm, and married his sweetheart, Vivian. Will Rogers dropped by the farm that fall to get a look at his replacement for Oklahoma's most famous citizen. Will was pleased and surprised to discover that Andy was the son of a man he knew, a man who had worked for Will's father many years before.

Deciding he might jog along in Will's famous footsteps for a lap or two, Andy tried his hand at entertaining and at newspaper writing. Neither of those careers was really to his liking, however, so in 1935 Andy decided to give politics a try. He got himself elected clerk of the Supreme Court of Oklahoma. When World War II came along, he went into the army for two years, and a grateful Governor Robert S. Kerr appointed Andy's wife to his job until he could get back home and take it up again. It

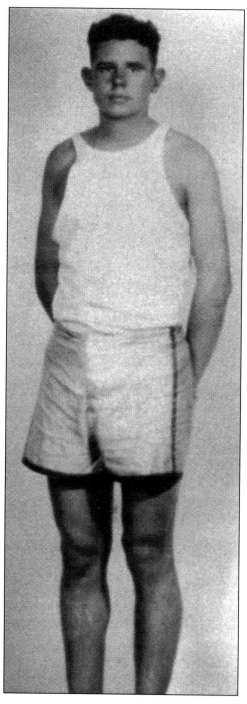

Andy Payne, winner of the Bunion Derby, in his running outfit.
—Vivian Payne collection

was the first time a woman had served as Supreme Court clerk, but by that time, folks in Oklahoma expected anybody named Payne to be first at anything they did.

Andy came back home from the war, went to law school, and ended up back clerking for the Oklahoma Supreme Court. He retired after thirty-eight years of service to his state.

His runner's heart gave out in 1977, but his spirit lives on in the many Bunion Derby marathon races that are run each year around the country.

Author's Note

Recorders of historical events are called upon to fit together many pieces of a story puzzle, usually when the edges of those pieces have been worn and nicked by years of use. Written records, no matter how reliable the source, often vary greatly, and personal interviews depend on memory, which sometimes slips and slides. The biographer, faced with having to sketch a scene in the stark gray and white of charcoal on paper, often chooses to color events a bit from his or her own private pallete of imagination.

I had the good fortune of being introduced to Andy Payne years ago, but that was long before I dreamed of writing the story of his amazing footrace. His death in 1977 not only diminished us all but also caused me to have to rely entirely on secondary sources. The Payne family was incredibly kind in sharing their printed and verbal treasures with Jim Ross and me. They also granted me the poetic license needed to tell Andy's story to young readers.

When it became necessary to blend facts into imaginary conversation, to put words into Andy's young mouth and thoughts into Andy's young head, I did so in a way I felt was true to his spirit and kind to his memory. After reading the manuscript, his daughter, Norma Roupe, said she felt her father would have approved of the portrait I painted of his biggest race. Her approval certainly warmed this non-runner's heart!

Fred Olds sculpture of Andy Payne located at the Cherokee Heritage Center outside Tahlequah, Oklahoma. A duplicate statue stands in Andy's hometown of Foyil.
—Courtesy Mark G. Lipe

About the Author

MOLLY LEVITE GRIFFIS of Norman, Oklahoma, began her writing career when she received her first diary for Christmas. Inspired by her no-nonsense, fact-finding father, who wrote for newspapers across Oklahoma, and her Texas-born-and-bred Mama, who spun the truth lightly on the tips of long red fingernails, Ms. Griffis is a master storyteller and word smith.

The author of five books, Ms. Griffis is a former teacher of English at all levels, from fourth grade through college. She is a graduate of the University of Oklahoma with a degree in speech, English, and creative writing and was a student of Foster Harris. She acted as a tour guide for the American Institute for Foreign Studies, where she designed a "Literary Tour of Europe." For nine years she owned her own publishing company, Levite of Apache.